# TREASURES OF MY MIND

# TREASURES OF MY MIND

*A Book of Quotations*

## KEITH SIMMONDS

**To order additional copies of this book, contact:**
Xlibris
1-888-795-4274
www.Xlibris.com
Orders@Xlibris.com
759989

# CONTENTS

# Foreword

Ever since I was a boy, I've enjoyed reading quotations. In a sense, I grew up on them, thanks to my grandmother, who, in spite of her home going may years ago, is still my favorite philosopher. From time to time I would frame my own and write them down in a notebook or even on a 3"x 5" card. Over time, I would reshape them and refine the thoughts behind the words. I still have a lot more to recover from missing notebooks and notecards and will perhaps rewrite, refine them as my life experiences have changed with the passage of time. I've been tempted to write an autobiography, but I'm not so sure that I have a comprehensive, continuous sense of myself, the way I do have of the periodic memories of my thoughts. In fact, a future publication might do better justice to the notion of **"treasures of my mind."**

We all evolve as human beings but not all of us pause to capture the key moments of our lives. It's a personal victory when an individual can bring together moments in time and key thoughts associated with those life experiences. At this point in time, I'll be content to simply share with my readers how I feel about aspects of life, such as life itself, love, family, social relationships, youth, education, self-improvement, society, politics, economics, and many more. Six plus decades of my life journey have left quite an impression on me. In some ways, those experiences have been stunning, even unbelievable; mostly good with noteworthy accomplishments, persistent love of family and lifelong friends. I consider life journey to have been a success, helped along the way by family members, mostly my wife, and children, well-wishers and even acquaintances. To them I will be eternally grateful; and they too will be everlasting **treasures of my mind.**

Having shared these sentiments with you, I invite you to come and let me share my thoughts with you.

## Life

God's greatest gift to humankind is life; humankind's show of appreciation is reproduction or extension of life.

## Life Activators

Patience, perseverance and persistence have been the triple generators of the light and love of my life. They teach me the lessons learned in life.

## Learning about life

I learn how to live life by watching others play it (in games or athletics).

## Price of Life

The price of life is death.

## Love

Love is complex yet simple; seek answers to its complexity but not at the expense of its simplicity

## Love team

Two heads are better than one; two hearts are warmer than one; two hands reach farther than one. A combination of all three contribute to a more fulfilled life.

## Vision

It's the blueprint for building a bridge to the future.

## Vision/mission

See it in your mind's eye first then actualize it.

## Joy

When the joy is gone it's time to move on. If you can't move on, stay on, and turn your daily lemons into refreshing lemonade.

## Caring and loving

Caring is the beginning of loving; loving is the beginning of sacrificing. When all three come together as one they exemplify the meaning of a beautiful human being.

## Daily Living

Live it, enjoy it, be at peace with it, and at the end pass on the benefits to those you would have left behind.

## Contrasts of natural Beauty

Be thankful for your "highs" and "lows." Have you ever stopped to wonder why the beautiful parts of this world are truly breathtaking? It's because of the natural contrasts of highs and lows, its narrows and widths, depths and shallows. They tell me something: If we are part of God's creation, the beauty in us will follow the same pattern of natural beauty. So take the (emotional) highs and lows with grace, because they are all evidence of the beauty, the greatness and the priceless worth in you.

## Secrets

It is those you tell your secrets to who might eventually tell on you. Think again before you allow your secrets to have double residency.

## Needs and wants

Focus on your needs and you'll be amazed how few your wants really are.

## Keeping grounded

I strive for 100% success in everything I do but often have to settle for a 90% outcome; the 10% shy of the mark keeps me grounded in reality and humble.

## Smile

Start your day with a smile; end it with a pleasant thought.

## Creation of Human Beings.
## The Big Question:

Are human beings the product of a divine purpose, or simply the outcome of a cosmic accident consisting of cosmic dust? I suppose it's the former, rather than the latter but we don't have access to the ladder that will enable us to reach over into the realm of cosmic understanding.

## Considered, measured opinion

If you can't quantify it, you can't measure it. If you can't measure it, you can't pass judgment on it; if you can't pass judgment on it, you can't be definitive about it; if you can't be definitive about it you won't have effective control over it. Therefore, as much as it is practical, always establish quantifiable, measurable criteria to govern your thoughts, actions and processes.

## Joy and Pain: Sides of Same Coin

Your joy could become the source of your pain. Ironically, though, your pain can be the good that came your way.

## Energy Investment

Invest your energy in what brings you joy.

## Joy and Happiness

Hold on to the joys of life; let go of the stresses of life.

## Guiding Stars

Learn to live and follow three guiding stars: love, compassion, and consideration for the feelings of others. By Love, be receptive to it, and be eager to share it. By compassion, have active empathy for those in need of compassion; be able to feel their pain and share in the efforts to relieve the pain. By consideration, be sensitive to the sensitivities of others. Be understanding of the shortcomings of others; be gentle where gentleness will engender self-empowerment of the person. Constantly apply the Golden Rule in your relationships with others.

## Reputation

You can't impress anyone of your great past, if your present is filled with unmistakable failure.

## Aim Right

Aim right, stay focused and you'll hit your target spot on!

## Recognition

There are those who have earned the right to be recognized but never received recognition. Then there are those who have been recognized but never earned the recognition.

## Youth

The Real Game.

The biggest game of all in America (especially for young people everywhere) is called "preparing for success." It involves preparing for tomorrow, selecting the choices that will increase one's earning potential, and converting earned income into wealth.

## Bad Habits

Stay away from self-destructive habits. They injure the body, disfigure the mind, and ultimately rob you of your precious life.

## Advice to Youth

You are on an exciting journey to a place where you will live for the rest of your life: it's called the future. Build a wonderful home there with lots of education, good character, great attitude, a high paying career, and a loving family of your own. Your mom and dad and siblings too, will be forever proud of you!

## Education

It's fuel for our children's racer cars; our youth are traveling as fast as they can into the future, often running on empty. Let's flag them down and get them to fill up at the next gas station called education. Let's fill their tanks with the highest possible octane. They'll be glad they took our advice!

## Learning and Earning

Learning comes before earning. To earn tomorrow, you must learn today.

## Education

What is the purpose of formal education? Is it transformational or just a commodity transferring cultural norms and stereotypes from one generation to another? I tried to make it transformational during my two years of middle school teaching and 31 years of higher education teaching.

## Early right start

Start early the right way, young people; you'll enjoy a long tomorrow.

## Inadequate knowledge

Is a robber of joy, disturber of the peace, and an obstacle to clear understanding.

## Communication skills

Good speaking comes from good reading and good writing comes from good thinking.

### Be careful!

Insistence on perfection is not always wise; eventually, it becomes the "enemy of the good."

### Meditation

Quiet meditation is a source of strength. Mindless noise is source of distraction.

## Make-believe

Unfortunately, a good portion of real life consists of genuine make-believe.

## The real question (about human behavior)

Don't ask me why the creator seemingly created humans with wide variations… some good, some bad, and some downright ugly in word and deed. That's not my worry. Ask me what can I do to help improve the human condition, starting with myself.

## Greed.

When greed surpasses need, your soul becomes the devil's feed.

## You're the Creator's "Linked-In"

The Creator talks to us through other people too; He shares His goodness and mercy with us and through us to others. We are the vessel; we must be prepared to let Him speak and act by having clean hands of delivery to our fellow human beings.

## Green Grass Syndrome

Don't let the green grass fool you; just seeing it and not walking through it could be deadly. Beware of the snakes lying there waiting to welcome you!

## Stay excited!

There are so many exciting things to see and do in this short span of life; just the thought of this reality is enough to keep me excited every day.

## Try Contentment!

A little can mean a lot if you enjoy much of the little you've got.

## Adversity

Every time adversity strikes, I improve.

## Self-Improvement

Keys to success

Passion, drive, commitment, enthusiasm and inspiration are excellent keys to success. Use them in combination with each other. Success may not mean ending up exactly where you originally intended to be, but you are guaranteed not to end up exactly where you started.

## Forgiveness

Forgiveness is all about "letting go" and "letting be."

## Forgiveness

Refusal to forgive builds up emotional plaque and before you know it, you'll experience coronary blockages of the soul, heart and mind. Avoid having to undergo multiple bypass of the mind.

## Criticism

Unfair criticism from a friend hurts more than flattery from a "frienemy" (non-genuine friend).

## Attitudes of the mind

Be always ready to transform your fear into faith, anxiety into hope, and dislikes into love. For the three greatest attitudes of the human mind are faith, hope and love.

## Self-direction

Don't let misguided or least informed people determine your choices in life. Study the "truth" of the matter, then decide.

## The Light of reassurance

Yes, indeed! Keep your eyes wide open in the darkness of despair; for sooner rather than later, the light of reassurance will shine through.

## Seek Help

Reach out for help from those you can trust; the result will be a happier mind, body and soul.

## Best formula for attitudinal adjustment

Learn to "unlove" a lot of people and things you once loved. Learn to love a lot of the people and things you once "unloved." It may require the following steps; first, admission that all is not well with you internally. Step two: dump the old disk drive that's contaminated with bad habits due to unhelpful thoughts; step three: install a new hard drive embedded in a powerful firewall to protect the new thoughts and actions flowing into the new drive. Step four: update your new drive regularly, checking and rechecking to make sure no corruptive viruses are entering your new mental hard drive. Step five: stay positive, regardless of the temptation (even justification) to go negative.

## Negative Vibes: Careful!

Jealousy and envy emanating from untested friends should make you feel like you're one step away from "sleeping" alligators. Beware!

## Happiness

Is a personal responsibility. Find or create a path that will increase your happiness daily. Then stay the course every day.

## Having the advantage

When you have the advantage, make sure you don't use it to the disadvantage of others.

## Contentment

Some people have to get it in bulk or in grand style to appreciate a gift. Others are just as thrilled with "a little today, the rest tomorrow." I grew up with the latter. I remember the parable of one stone at a time thrown in the half pitcher of water. Each day the water rose a little higher and higher, until the wood pecker was able to quench its thirst. Over my life time, my needs got met; those not met were filled by contentment.

## Attitude

Oh how much we lose depending on the attitude we choose.

## Prescription for a happy life

Live simply

Live reverently

Live sensibly

Live joyfully, and

Dedicate your life to improving the human condition (i.e. the life circumstances of human beings)

## Politics, economics and democracy

Politics is a civil activity intended to legitimize the acquisition, distribution, control or management of a nation's resources. Those who own the resources generally organize and develop structures with procedures that facilitate continuity or change in the control or management of resources. An economic system is the underpinning of political activity. Together, politics and economics fuse themselves into a philosophy, called democracy, intended to explain and validate the nation's twin political and economic behaviors.

## Politics

Democracy

It describes the philosophy of so-called democratic countries. It is, as a matter of consequence, a pretense of interaction between the owners of (significant) wealth and strivers of wealth (i.e. the laboring masses of the nation). This interaction indicates, even encourages citizen participation in electoral procedures and even active civic engagement in the political process. Such engagement supposedly accommodates change of leadership among the owners and managers of the nation's wealth

## Political mind control

I can hear that cynical politian behind closed doors during an election campaign, saying: If I can control the voters' mind I sure will be able to control their voting behavior. How true: teach me how to think, soon I'll behave the way you wish.

## Political seduction

Seduction and deception are critical elements of politics; he or she who doesn't understand this is not ready to see the political power plays and to predict their outcome.

## Management vs. Leadership

Management is doing what is designed to be done; leadership is creating what is to be done. Leadership requires vision, mission and direction if it is to be distinguished from management.

## Societal Leaders

The designers of what we call "civilized society" pretty much got it wrong; it's just that over time the ordinary man and woman got socialized into thinking that they, the designers, got it right. Sorry, I don't believe they did.

## Criminal justice in America

Some folks commit a crime and go to jail; others commit a crime, avoid jail and write a book about it, laughing all the way to the bank. Must be nice!

## Good managers

Good managers are governed by four principles and insist on their subordinates governing themselves accordingly. These are professionalism, productivity, purposeful loyalty, punctuality and focused commitment. Optimal efficiency and effectiveness are sure to follow.

## Game of Politics

Still a rich man's game; or a battle ground of the power hungry.

## Responsibility of political leadership

Political leaders in Less Developed Countries (LDC): Ask not what your citizens can do for you; ask what you can do for your citizens, as they seek to give back to their country.

## Leadership

Leadership is everything, yet its weakest link is followership. Leadership without solidarity followership, will soon fall apart.

## Protest marches

Don't just march, organize; build from the base and run for office; get elected and coalesce with others in politics, and make a difference.

## Money and politics

Money and power, as well as the desire to control both, are at the heart of all political and economic relationships, or their structural settings.

## Political dominance

Persistent white control of the political and economic system of the US is secured by the electoral process of Winner-Takes-All. Its future, though, is uncertain as the demographics of the country tilt toward a majority of minority complexion. I fear the hand writing is on the wall.

## Life's unfair

Everyday politics reveals the unfairness of life: the rich stay wealthy because of the poor; the knowledgeable people stay one step ahead of the ignorant, and exploit their ignorance; in so doing they reinforce their privilege, power and position.

## Effective national leadership

Qualities of effective leadership include: responsible acquisition of relevant resources, access, use and responsible distribution of resources; effective organization; securing joint public-private partnerships; initiative and individual responsibility of citizens.

## Poverty

### Poverty guaranteed

1. Give what you don't have
2. Give without asking back for it
3. Lend without seeking to be repaid
4. Live beyond your means
5. Be content with a salaried income
6. Never seek to invest portions of your income

Follow these six behaviors and you'll stay forever poor.

## Keeping My Distance

As for me, all I want of poverty is to keep it at a permanent distance, having it watching my back and the soles of my feet in motion.

## Man's greatest treasure

Time is precious; manage it wisely.

## Problems

Problems are the perceptions and definitions of the mind. Redefine the perception, you may very well have solved the perceived problem.

## True problem solving

If you cannot solve a problem learn to contain it, manage it and, if necessary, be content with it.

## Manage your expectations

Tone down your own expectations, in most things. Most times we really overextend ourselves, unnecessarily.

## Perceptions

You are what you think; your perception of others is essentially the definition of your mind.

## Don't worry

Turn your worries into aspirations.

## Healthy Relationships

A relationship without passion or continual renewal of itself soon loses its glow and its hope. Eventually, it will fade away.

## My definition of a serious academic (a professional in the academy)

It is that person (male or female) who rigorously explores knowledge; effectively communicates it; regularly contributes to the body of knowledge of the academic discipline. The academic also has a human side to his professional life: he gives a hand to those needing an outstretched hand; he's a voice for the voiceless; a pathfinder for those seeking the door of opportunity. Lastly, he does what he can to make the journey of life a little easier for all.

## Two-fold Thankfulness

Don't be stingy with your Thanksgiving. Don't just give thanks for having lived to see another day. But give thanks for good health and strength that came with it. And most of all give thanks for being able to know who you are and where you are, upon rising to witness a fresh day of life. To be alive and not know it is one of life's saddest state of being.

## Age imposed limits

You know that life for you has changed when you're limited to half of everything you still enjoy. Like half a cup of coffee instead of the whole cup. I can list 101 other things! Like half a good time instead of enjoying it all night long.

## Kindness

Kindness has its dangers. There is kindness - without affection, and kindness - with affection. The danger is that the first can transform into the latter. When that happens and a falling out takes place, hatred between the giver and recipient of kindness can become real intense, even deadly.

## Cracks in my perfection (personality)

The (minor) cracks in my personality cause me at times to jump the tracks of rationality. Except for those rare times, I'm one of God's finest human beings to have been created.

## Mental compartmentalization

Learn to compartmentalize your mind. You can multitask better and enable your consciousness to prioritize optimally throughout the day.

## Wisdom

You are blessed with wisdom if you know the difference between a dream delayed and a dream denied. Chances are, your set back is just a dream delayed. Stay the course for faith, patience, and self-confidence will see you through.

## Words of Grandma

"Siddung never say get up." Meaning: you may feel so good sitting down, you just don't feel like getting up, especially when you know you need to get up and get going. A feeling of physical tiredness led to her sitting down, yet the work had to be done, "so get up, oh tired soul," she would say.

## Grandma's Advice

My Grandma use to tell me: If you go looking for trouble you'll find it; so be wise and stay away from it. Since then, I've added to that by saying, if you go looking for unhappiness you'll find it, so be wise and stay away from unhappy people, places and things.

## Doing the right thing

I use subjective criteria to make that determination: If what you do

1. hurts no one
2. harms no one
3. disadvantages no one
4. undignifies no one
5. leads to mutual benefit
6. and is of mutual consent

Do it and move one.

## Focus

Stay focused. Keep your eyes on the ball and fix your mind on the goal.

## Many Lives in One

Life consists of many lives. Choose the one that's filled with joy and laughter.

## Destination

Certainty of direction will get you to your pre-planned direction. Uncertainty will require stop-and-go and possibly ending up anywhere.

## Social partnerships

If you are satisfied with the Biblical (New Testament) notion of monogamy, you should live faithfully to that precept. If you are satisfied with the Koran's (or other religious) sanctions of polygamy, then pursue it and live it faithfully. If you, as an individual, are desirous of a more customized formula of "committed partnership," so long as both (or all) parties benefit and it's a win - win for all, live the commitment faithfully and joyfully. Enjoy your life the way you see fit so long as you treat your partner(s) the way you would like to be treated.

## At the end of a rough day

I'm comforted by the thought: I'm still here, fueled with hope, and driven by His goodness to me.

## Also…

Let the billows roll and winds overpower the sea, let the affliction sting, bite and knife me,

I'll still be ready for the next day.

## Disguised blessings

Blessed are the rocky roads and thunder storms of life;
they make you tougher, stronger, and wiser.

## Wealth

There is no greater wealth than good health and a peace
of mind.

## Tune-in, Tune-out

Tune-in to the quietness within; tune-out the noise around you.

## Sacrifice

Sacrifice is temporary; success is permanent.

## Be practical

Free your mind of things not practical; fill the void with contentment and gratitude

## Reverence for the Creator

Reverence for the Creator is the beginning of wisdom. Avoidance of or departure from self-destructive choices is evidence of wisdom.

## Looking Back

**You've come a long way baby!**

Rejoice and be glad, you are way ahead of the pack. Just look back for a moment and you'll see the pack and the distance from where you started.

## Rear mirror view

Looking back over my life I can see five fairly distinct yet overlapping phases of my life's journey: the first were my boyhood and teenage years, filled with a lot of religious activities; the second, my college years, laying down the foundation for a professional career; third phase, actual building of a professional career and starting a family; fourth phase consisted of solidifying professional career and family life; the fifth included drawing benefits from career activities and enjoying family life; and if there is to be a sixth, it will be a matter of "just chilling," relaxing and enjoying life in the departure lounge of life.

## At 50

I remember well at age 50 I said, from here on out the focus of my time would be to pull back from the pressure of building and maintaining a successful career. Put the energy into lending a hand to those who need a hand, be a voice for the voiceless and be a light to those who need one as he or she makes it through life. I've kept that focus in more ways than one and for that I'm happy.

## Ten years on

I'm just chilling, with the attitude of "live and let live;" and still be a hand to those who need one, when I can, and be that voice showing support for the underserved and underrepresented.

## What's Next?

It seems all but settled in terms of what I want to do in the outlying years. Preferences will include: become a serious author; become an effective counselor; do more international service travel; and spend much more time with family I love dearly and those who truly love me.